# 21 PERSONAL BREAKTHROUGH PRAYERS & SCRIPTURES

*Removing*
*Longstanding Obstacles*

LIFE IMPACT SERIES

# FRANK DAMAZIO

CityChristianPublishing

www.CityChristianPublishing.com

PUBLISHED BY CITY CHRISTIAN PUBLISHING
9200 NE Fremont, Portland, Oregon 97220

City Christian Publishing is a ministry of City Bible Church and is dedicated to serving the local church and its leaders through the production and distribution of quality equipping resources. It is our prayer that these materials, proven in the context of the local church, will equip leaders in exalting the Lord and extending His kingdom.

For a free catalog of additional resources from City Christian Publishing, please call 1-800-777-6057 or visit our web site at www.CityChristianPublishing.com.

**21 Personal Breakthrough Prayers & Scriptures**

ISBN: 978-1-59383-076-2
Cover design by DesignPoint, Inc.
Interior design and typeset by City Christian Publishing.

All Scripture quotations, unless otherwise indicated, are taken from the *New King James Version*. Copyright © 1979, 1980, 1982 by Thomas Nelson, Inc. Publishers. Used by permission. All rights reserved.

**First Edition, July 2006**

Printed in the United States of America

# Table of Contents

## WEEK ONE
### Prayers for Blessing and Favor

## WEEK TWO
### Prayers for New Spiritual Power

# WEEK THREE
## Prayers for Fresh Anointing

# 21 Personal Breakthrough Prayers & Scriptures

# Introduction

Some say that it takes 21 days to break a bad habit or to form a new habit. I believe this same principle can apply to overcoming obstacles and achieving personal breakthroughs. The obstacles we face may be broken relationships, health problems, job insecurity, financial troubles, concerns about the future, doubts about our faith, temptations we can't seem to overcome, foundless fears, or any number of situations. The key to breakthrough in these areas? Taking them to God.

The 21 prayers and scriptures in this book will help you create a closer relationship and communication with God. God wants to hear your concerns, but he also wants to reveal a message to you. He wants you to experience breakthrough in your spirit, in your soul, in your family, in your relationships, in your finances, and your job. He wants to renew your vision and dreams. He wants to renew heart in those who have lost heart. He also wants to remove the cynicism that would have you say, "I've done this before and nothing happened." That's the enemy dropping his seeds of doubt. The Holy Spirit is not a doubter. The Holy Spirit says, "This is a new time."

God can work a miracle in your life. God can work a miracle in your circumstance. Jeremiah 33:3 says: "Call to me and I will answer you." We could all use a few answers—answers to prayers and answers to questions. "I will answer you," God promises. But God doesn't stop there. He adds: "And I will show you great and mighty things."

I find that the more I live in myself, the more I live with worldly energy and thoughts. When I believe as the world does that only those things I see, smell, touch, and hear are real, the less I think about great and mighty things. I settle for little and weak things. Little prayers. Weak living. Little answers.

If I allow myself to be away from prayer and away from the Word and away from the invisible Kingdom of God, I don't see the possibilities. Only through prayer and the Word can we touch the real world, which is the spiritual world, the world that God rules, the world that God moves in, the world that is faith-filled and miracle-filled. That world has a lot of different ideas in it: Nothing is impossible. All things are possible. I will answer you. *Great and mighty things.*

This can be just another year in your life or it can be a great and mighty year, a time of personal breakthrough. The essence of breakthrough is trusting and believing that God is in control and that He is Lord, and all things are working together every day for your good.

I strongly recommend that you read aloud both the prayers and the scriptures presented in this book. Speaking the words rather than passively reading them brings action and power to the prayers and verses, a power that dissolves bonds and breaks down obstacles. Take time to listen, too. God wants to bring you a message and wants you to know there is an appointed time for that message.

I pray this three-week focus on breakthrough will transform your life, your relationships, and your future for the glory of God. I pray you will grow in favor and encounter miracles and that God will pour out blessings and favor throughout your life.

# Day One

## *Blessing and Favor upon My Year*

In Jesus' name, by the power of the blood shed on the cross, by the authority of the scriptures, I proclaim a mighty blessing upon my life, my now, and my future, and all that pertains to my life, my health, my home, my finances, my friends, and my church. I proclaim this year to be a year of favor, blessing, new spiritual power, increase, expansion, fresh anointing, and great personal breakthrough for the glory of God.

## Deuteronomy 11:8-15

*Therefore you shall keep every commandment which I command you today, that you may be strong, and go in and possess the land which you cross over to possess, and that you may prolong your days in the land which the LORD swore to give your fathers, to them and their descendants, 'a land flowing with milk and honey.' For the land which you go to possess is not like the land of Egypt from which you have come, where you sowed your seed and watered it by foot, as a vegetable garden; but the land which you cross over to possess is a land of hills and valleys, which drinks water from the rain of heaven, a land for which the LORD your God cares; the eyes of the LORD your God are always on it, from the beginning of the year to the very end of the year. 'And it shall be that if you earnestly obey My commandments which I command you today, to love the LORD your God and serve Him with all your heart and with all your soul, then I will give you the rain for your land in its season, the early rain and the latter rain, that you may gather in your grain, your new wine, and your oil. And I will send grass in your fields for your livestock, that you may eat and be filled.'*

## Psalm 5:11-12

But let all those rejoice who put their trust in You; Let them ever shout for joy, because You defend them; Let those also who love Your name be joyful in You. For You, O LORD, will bless the righteous; with favor You will surround him as with a shield.

## Psalm 65:9-13

You visit the earth and water it, You greatly enrich it; The river of God is full of water; You provide their grain, for so You have prepared it. You water its ridges abundantly, You settle its furrows; You make it soft with showers, You bless its growth. You crown the year with Your goodness, and Your paths drip with abundance. They drop on the pastures of the wilderness, and the little hills rejoice on every side. The pastures are clothed with flocks; the valleys also are covered with grain; they shout for joy, they also sing.

## Psalm 102:12-18

But You, O LORD, shall endure forever, and the remembrance of Your name to all generations. You will arise and have mercy on Zion; for the time to favor her, Yes, the set time, has come. For Your servants take pleasure in her stones, and show favor to her dust. So the nations shall fear the name of the LORD, and all the kings of the earth Your glory. For the LORD shall build up Zion; He shall appear in His glory. He shall regard the prayer of the destitute, and shall not despise their prayer. This will be written for the generation to come, that a people yet to be created may praise the LORD.

## Proverbs 3:1-4

My son, do not forget my law, but let your heart keep my commands; for length of days and long life and peace they will add to you. Let not mercy and truth forsake you; bind them around your neck, write them on the tablet of your heart, and so find favor and high esteem in the sight of God and man.

## Lamentations 3:21-25

This I recall to my mind, therefore I have hope. Through the LORD's mercies we are not consumed, because His compassions fail not. They are new every morning; great is Your faithfulness. "The LORD is my portion," says my soul, "Therefore I hope in Him!" The LORD is good to those who wait for Him, to the soul who seeks Him.

## Joel 2:23-26

*Be glad then, you children of Zion, and rejoice in the LORD your God; for He has given you the former rain faithfully, and He will cause the rain to come down for you—the former rain, and the latter rain in the first month. The threshing floors shall be full of wheat, and the vats shall overflow with new wine and oil. "So I will restore to you the years that the swarming locust has eaten, the crawling locust, the consuming locust, and the chewing locust, my great army which I sent among you. You shall eat in plenty and be satisfied, and praise the name of the LORD your God, who has dealt wondrously with you; and My people shall never be put to shame.*

# Day Two

## *Blessing and Favor Upon My Life*

I stand in awe of Your faithful and merciful hand upon my life. Year after year, You are my hope, my future, and my anchor. I believe Your word that says Your eyes are always upon me and upon my year and years to come. From the beginning of the year to the end of the year, You watch over every step I take, every prayer I pray, every trial I encounter. You fill my every day with Your presence. You crown my year with Your goodness. My paths drip with abundance. My decisions are protected by Your grace and mercy. Your hand of blessing and favor rests mightily upon me this year. You surround me like a shield and defend me from my enemies. I know You have planned great things for my life, and my future is awesome because of You!

## Psalm 84:11

*For the LORD God is a sun and shield; the LORD will give grace and glory; no good thing will He withhold from those who walk uprightly.*

## Jeremiah 29:11

*For I know the thoughts that I think toward you, says the LORD, thoughts of peace and not of evil, to give you a future and a hope.*

## Proverbs 8:32-36

*Now therefore, listen to me, my children, for blessed are those who keep my ways. Hear instruction and be wise, and do not disdain it. Blessed is the man who listens to me, watching daily at my gates, waiting at the posts of my doors. For whoever finds me finds life, and obtains favor from the LORD; but he who sins against me wrongs his own soul; all those who hate me love death."*

## 1 Chronicles 4:10

*And Jabez called on the God of Israel saying, "Oh, that You would bless me indeed, and enlarge my territory, that Your* hand would be with me, and that You would keep me from evil, that I may not cause pain!" So God granted him what he requested.

## Ezra 8:23

So we fasted and entreated our God for this,
and He answered our prayer.

## Genesis 32:24-26

Then Jacob was left alone; and a Man wrestled with him until the breaking of day. Now when He saw that He did not prevail against him, He touched the socket of his hip; and the socket of Jacob's hip was out of joint as He wrestled with him. And He said, "Let Me go, for the day breaks." But he said, "I will not let You go unless You bless me!"

# Day Three

## *Blessing and Favor on My Finances*

Thank You Lord, that I have received instructions from your word on how to order my finances. I am blessed so that I can be a blessing to my family, my friends, my church, and my world. I have made the decision to put You first in my life as well as my finances. I have committed my first 10 percent to You all the days of my life and from my surplus, I will be liberal and generous. I thank You for Your faithful provision, for the windows of heaven being opened over my life, for the barns filled with plenty, for the pressing down and overflowing of Your amazing blessings. The continued force of your blessings has created a supernatural breakthrough in my finances. Thank You Lord, for the flow of Your grace toward my life.

## Genesis 17:1

*When Abram was ninety-nine years old, the LORD appeared to Abram and said to him, "I am Almighty God; walk before Me and be blameless.*

## Genesis 22:14

*And Abraham called the name of the place, The-LORD-Will-Provide; as it is said to this day, "In the Mount of the LORD it shall be provided."*

## Matthew 6:19-21

*Do not lay up for yourselves treasures on earth, where moth and rust destroy and where thieves break in and steal; but lay up for yourselves treasures in heaven, where neither moth nor rust destroys and where thieves do not break in and steal. For where your treasure is, there your heart will be also.*

## Deuteronomy 28:12

*The LORD will open to you His good treasure, the heavens, to give the rain to your land in its season, and to bless all the* work of your hand. You shall lend to many nations, but you shall not borrow.

## Malachi 3:10

"Bring all the tithes into the storehouse, that there may be food in My house, and try Me now in this," says the LORD of hosts, "If I will not open for you the windows of heaven and pour out for you such blessing that there will not be room enough to receive it."

## Philippians 4:6, 19

Be anxious for nothing, but in everything by prayer and supplication, with thanksgiving, let your requests be made known to God; . . . And my God shall supply all your need according to His riches in glory by Christ Jesus.

## Luke 6:38

Give, and it will be given to you: good measure, pressed down, shaken together, and running over will be put into your bosom. For with the same measure that you use, it will be measured back to you.

## Proverbs 3:9-10

*Honor the LORD with your possessions, and with the first-fruits of all your increase; so your barns will be filled with plenty, and your vats will overflow with new wine.*

## Proverbs 11:24-25

*There is one who scatters, yet increases more; and there is one who withholds more than is right, but it leads to poverty. The generous soul will be made rich, and he who waters will also be watered himself.*

# Day Four

## *Blessing and Favor on My Faith*

I thank you Lord for the courage to stand on my faith and to use my faith as You create power in and around my life. Lord, give me resoluteness in my standing on Your word, confidence to take heart in the dark hours of life and faith to persevere against all odds. Do not let me faint in the day of adversity, lose heart, or become fainthearted. Let me look in the face of danger and be persuaded that You are able to do exceedingly, abundantly above all that I ask or ever imagine. You are able! You are my God! My life is in Your hands and I trust You absolutely. I will not be moved from my ground of faith. Lord, give me the faith that receives everything I need, faith that triumphs over everything I face, and faith that finishes the race You have set before me.

Let my faith generate spiritual breakthrough: a faith that sees the invisible, believes the incredible, and receives the impossible.

## John 14:12-15

*Most assuredly, I say to you, he who believes in Me, the works that I do he will do also; and greater works than these he will do, because I go to My Father. And whatever you ask in My name, that I will do, that the Father may be glorified in the Son. If you ask anything in My name, I will do it. If you love Me, keep My commandments."*

## Luke 18:27

*But He said, "The things which are impossible with men are possible with God."*

## Proverbs 10:22

*The blessing of the LORD makes one rich, and He adds no sorrow with it.*

## Psalms 37:4

*Delight yourself also in the LORD, and He shall give you the desires of your heart.*

## Hebrews 11:1

*Now faith is the substance of things hoped for, the evidence of things not seen.*

## Mark 11:22-24

*So Jesus answered and said to them, "Have faith in God. For assuredly, I say to you, whoever says to this mountain, 'Be removed and be cast into the sea,' and does not doubt in his heart, but believes that those things he says will be done, he will have whatever he says. Therefore I say to you, whatever things you ask when you pray, believe that you receive them, and you will have them.*

## Numbers 13:20

*Whether the land is rich or poor; and whether there are forests there or not. Be of good courage. And bring some of the fruit of the land. Now the time was the season of the first ripe grapes.*

## 2 Corinthians 4:16

*Therefore we do not lose heart. Even though our outward man is perishing, yet the inward man is being renewed day by day.*

## Luke 18:1

*Then He spoke a parable to them that men always ought to pray and not lose heart.*

# Day Five

## *Blessing and Favor on My Marriage and Family*

Lord, I pray You deliver my soul from the lies and attacks of the enemy that would sow wrong thoughts or wrong thinking that causes a wrong perspective on my marriage. I align myself to Your word, O Lord. Your word confirms marriage to be holy and a God-made institution, a marriage between one man and one woman, a marriage that is to last a lifetime, a marriage that is to bring forth children who will become a blessing. Lord, I believe that even my worst days are never so bad that you cannot reach into my marriage and change me, make me, and restore me. Lord, bless my marriage, my children, and children's children. Lord, provide that right mate for my children. Lord, bless every area of my life and my marriage, my family, my home. Create a momentum within our family tree that will carry the blessing of a godly marriage and family.

## Genesis 2:18-25

*And the LORD God said, "It is not good that man should be alone; I will make him a helper comparable to him." Out of the ground the LORD God formed every beast of the field and every bird of the air, and brought them to Adam to see what he would call them. And whatever Adam called each living creature, that was its name. So Adam gave names to all cattle, to the birds of the air, and to every beast of the field. But for Adam there was not found a helper comparable to him. And the LORD God caused a deep sleep to fall on Adam, and he slept; and He took one of his ribs, and closed up the flesh in its place. Then the rib which the LORD God had taken from man He made into a woman, and He brought her to the man. And Adam said: "This is now bone of my bones and flesh of my flesh; she shall be called Woman, because she was taken out of Man." Therefore a man shall leave his father and mother and be joined to his wife, and they shall become one flesh. And they were both naked, the man and his wife, and were not ashamed.*

## Malachi 2:14

*Yet you say, "For what reason?" Because the LORD has been witness between you and the wife of your youth, with whom you have dealt treacherously; yet she is your companion and your wife by covenant.*

## Proverbs 5:18

*Let your fountain be blessed, and rejoice with the wife of your youth.*

## Isaiah 59:19

*So shall they fear the name of the LORD from the west, and His glory from the rising of the sun; when the enemy comes in like a flood, the Spirit of the LORD will lift up a standard against him.*

## Psalms 127:1-3

*Unless the LORD builds the house, they labor in vain who build it; unless the LORD guards the city, the watchman stays awake in vain. It is vain for you to rise up early, to sit up late, to eat the bread of sorrows; for so He gives His be-*

loved sleep. Behold, children are a heritage from the LORD, the fruit of the womb is a reward.

## Isaiah 52:12-13

For you shall not go out with haste, nor go by flight; for the LORD will go before you, and the God of Israel will be your rear guard. Behold, My Servant shall deal prudently; He shall be exalted and extolled and be very high.

## Proverbs 31:10

Who can find a virtuous wife? For her worth is far above rubies.

## Ephesians 2:10

For we are His workmanship, created in Christ Jesus for good works, which God prepared beforehand that we should walk in them.

## *Ecclesiastes 4:9-12*

*Two are better than one, because they have a good reward for their labor. For if they fall, one will lift up his companion. But woe to him who is alone when he falls, for he has no one to help him up. Again, if two lie down together, they will keep warm; but how can one be warm alone? Though one may be overpowered by another, two can withstand him. And a threefold cord is not quickly broken.*

# Day Six

## *Blessing and Favor on My Work*

Lord, today I ask specifically that You bless the work of my hands; bless and put Your favor upon my job, my business, my career. Teach me to work heartily as unto You, not man. Teach me to put my whole heart and soul into my work, to serve with integrity, to obey and respect those over me, and to make the business prosper. Lord, give me a diligent heart at and for my work, a working hand with careful effort attitude. Help me to be industrious, accomplishing what my responsibility requires of me. Lord, I know You desire to bless and prosper me in my work, to help me provide new ideas and create a personal breakthrough around my job, my business, my world of work. Lord, let me remember You have redeemed my work from the curse and that work under the Lordship of Christ can be fulfilling, satisfying, and exciting, bringing glory to You. Thank you Lord, for what You are about to do in and through my work.

## Colossians 3:23-24

*And whatever you do, do it heartily, as to the Lord and not to men, knowing that from the Lord you will receive the reward of the inheritance; for you serve the Lord Christ.*

## Ephesians 6:5-8

*Bondservants, be obedient to those who are your masters according to the flesh, with fear and trembling, in sincerity of heart, as to Christ; not with eye service, as men-pleasers, but as bondservants of Christ, doing the will of God from the heart, with goodwill doing service, as to the Lord, and not to men, knowing that whatever good anyone does, he will receive the same from the Lord, whether he is a slave or free.*

## Proverbs 10:4

*He who has a slack hand becomes poor, but the hand of the diligent makes rich.*

## Proverbs 21:5

*The plans of the diligent lead surely to plenty, but those of everyone who is hasty, surely to poverty.*

## Romans 12:11

*Not lagging in diligence, fervent in spirit, serving the Lord.*

## I Peter 5:6-7

*Therefore humble yourselves under the mighty hand of God, that He may exalt you in due time, casting all your care upon Him, for He cares for you.*

## Proverbs 14:23

*In all labor there is profit, but idle chatter leads only to poverty.*

## Proverbs 27:18

*Whoever keeps the fig tree will eat its fruit; so he who waits on his master will be honored.*

## Proverbs 10:22

*The blessing of the LORD makes one rich, and He adds no sorrow with it.*

## Deuteronomy 28:3-6

*Blessed shall you be in the city, and blessed shall you be in the country. Blessed shall be the fruit of your body, the produce of your ground and the increase of your herds, the increase of your cattle and the offspring of your flocks. Blessed shall be your basket and your kneading bowl. Blessed shall you be when you come in, and blessed shall you be when you go out.*

# Day Seven

## *Blessing and Favor on My Thinking*

Lord, I pray that You would help me align my thought life to You, Your word, and Your Holy Spirit. I know my thoughts will determine the level of my spiritual health and ultimately my spiritual destiny. Lord, teach me to weigh my thoughts and choose those thoughts that are pure and pleasing to You. Help me Lord to win the battle over the evil or dark thoughts the enemy desires to throw toward my mind. Lord, teach me and enable me to control my thinking, to guard my thoughts, and to resist the enemy of my soul. Convert my mind, alter, and mold my mind according to Your word. Create in me a new thought process, a new thought discipline. Let there be a breakthrough in me to renew my mind and think the thoughts of You!

## Romans 12:3

*For I say, through the grace given to me, to everyone who is among you, not to think of himself more highly than he ought to think, but to think soberly, as God has dealt to each one a measure of faith.*

## 2 Timothy 1:7

*For God has not given us a spirit of fear, but of power and of love and of a sound mind.*

## Philippians 4:7

*And the peace of God, which surpasses all understanding, will guard your hearts and minds through Christ Jesus.*

## 1 Peter 1:13

*Therefore gird up the loins of your mind, be sober, and rest your hope fully upon the grace that is to be brought to you at the revelation of Jesus Christ.*

## Psalms 51:6

Behold, You desire truth in the inward parts, and in the hidden part You will make me to know wisdom.

## Galatians 5:1

Stand fast therefore in the liberty by which Christ has made us free, and do not be entangled again with a yoke of bondage.

## Hebrews 12:1

Therefore we also, since we are surrounded by so great a cloud of witnesses, let us lay aside every weight, and the sin which so easily ensnares us, and let us run with endurance the race that is set before us.

## 2 Corinthians 11:3

But I fear, lest somehow, as the serpent deceived Eve by his craftiness, so your minds may be corrupted from the simplicity that is in Christ.

## 2 Corinthians 10:4-5

*For the weapons of our warfare are not carnal but mighty in God for pulling down strongholds, casting down arguments and every high thing that exalts itself against the knowledge of God, bringing every thought into captivity to the obedience of Christ.*

## Matthew 15:19

*For out of the heart proceed evil thoughts, murders, adulteries, fornications, thefts, false witness, blasphemies.*

## Ephesians 6:10-13

*Finally, my brethren, be strong in the Lord and in the power of His might. Put on the whole armor of God, that you may be able to stand against the wiles of the devil. For we do not wrestle against flesh and blood, but against principalities, against powers, against the rulers of the darkness of this age, against spiritual hosts of wickedness in the heavenly places. Therefore take up the whole armor of God, that you may be able to withstand in the evil day, and having done all, to stand.*

## Colossians 3:1-2

*If then you were raised with Christ, seek those things which are above, where Christ is, sitting at the right hand of God. Set your mind on things above, not on things on the earth.*

# Day Eight

## *New Spiritual Power to Resist the Enemy*

Lord, grant me the spiritual understanding of how I can resist the devil. I have faith and I stand against the enemy through the power of Jesus' name. God is my shield and my refuge, a very present help in time of trouble. When the enemy comes against my soul, the Holy Spirit will raise a standard against Him. The Lord will be my strength and I shall not be moved. I shall stand my ground in the day of battle. When my soul is attacked by a series of unusual bad experiences, irritations, and small calamities, I will resist the devil's lies by standing with my spiritual armor. I shall not be moved, for greater is He who is in me than He that is in the world. I pray the word of God. I submit to You, O Lord. I resist the devil and I demand that He flee from me. I draw near to You, Lord, with a pure heart and a faith in Your power.

## James 4:7-8

*Therefore submit to God. Resist the devil and he will flee from you. Draw near to God and He will draw near to you. Cleanse your hands, you sinners; and purify your hearts, you double-minded.*

## 1 Peter 5:8-9

*Be sober, be vigilant; because your adversary the devil walks about like a roaring lion, seeking whom he may devour. Resist him, steadfast in the faith, knowing that the same sufferings are experienced by your brotherhood in the world.*

## Leviticus 26:8

*Five of you shall chase a hundred, and a hundred of you shall put ten thousand to flight; your enemies shall fall by the sword before you.*

## 2 Corinthians 2:11

*Lest Satan should take advantage of us; for we are not ignorant of his devices.*

## Genesis 49:22-24

*Joseph is a fruitful bough, a fruitful bough by a well; his branches run over the wall. The archers have bitterly grieved him, shot at him and hated him. But his bow remained in strength, and the arms of his hands were made strong by the hands of the Mighty God of Jacob (from there is the Shepherd, the Stone of Israel).*

## Ephesians 6:11-18

*Put on the whole armor of God, that you may be able to stand against the wiles of the devil. For we do not wrestle against flesh and blood, but against principalities, against powers, against the rulers of the darkness of this age, against spiritual hosts of wickedness in the heavenly places. Therefore take up the whole armor of God, that you may be able to withstand in the evil day, and having done all, to stand. Stand therefore, having girded your waist with truth, having put on the breastplate of righteousness, and having shod your feet with the preparation of the gospel of peace; above all, taking the shield of faith with which you will be able to quench all the fiery darts of the wicked one. And take the helmet of salvation, and the sword of the Spirit, which is the* word of God; praying always with all prayer and supplication in the Spirit, being watchful to this end with all perseverance and supplication for all the saints.

## Isaiah 54:17

No weapon formed against you shall prosper, and every tongue which rises against you in judgment You shall condemn. This is the heritage of the servants of the LORD, and their righteousness is from Me," says the LORD.

## I John 4:4

You are of God, little children, and have overcome them, because He who is in you is greater than he who is in the world.

## Revelation 12:9-11

So the great dragon was cast out, that serpent of old, called the Devil and Satan, who deceives the whole world; he was cast to the earth, and his angels were cast out with him. Then I heard a loud voice saying in heaven, "Now salvation, and strength, and the kingdom of our God, and the power of

*His Christ have come, for the accuser of our brethren, who accused them before our God day and night, has been cast down. And they overcame him by the blood of the Lamb and by the word of their testimony, and they did not love their lives to the death.*

## Colossians 2:15

*Having disarmed principalities and powers, He made a public spectacle of them, triumphing over them in it.*

## Deuteronomy 28:7

*The LORD will cause your enemies who rise against you to be defeated before your face; they shall come out against you one way and flee before you seven ways.*

## Psalms 34:7

*The angel of the LORD encamps all around those who fear Him, and delivers them.*

# Day Nine

## *New Spiritual Power to Stand in the Gap*

Today, Lord, I respond to the call of the spirit to become a gap-standing prayer person, to be prepared and equipped by the Holy Spirit to intercede with power and stand in the gap for the many needs that I see arise. Holy Spirit, come and fill me, anoint me and guide me in prayer intercession, for You are the best prayer partner. You know exactly what to pray and how to pray. Come partner with me today, fill my mouth with Your words for You know the end from the beginning. You know the will of God in every circumstance. I choose today to stand in the gap and persistently call on the name of the

Lord with a fervent spirit petitioning You with an all-consuming passion, centered immovably upon Your word. Lord, create a powerful prayer breakthrough in and around my life.

## Ezekiel 22:30-31

*"So I sought for a man among them who would make a wall, and stand in the gap before Me on behalf of the land, that I should not destroy it; but I found no one. Therefore I have poured out My indignation on them; I have consumed them with the fire of My wrath; and I have recompensed their deeds on their own heads," says the Lord GOD.*

## Ezekiel 13:4-5

*O Israel, your prophets are like foxes in the deserts. You have not gone up into the gaps to build a wall for the house of Israel to stand in battle on the day of the LORD.*

## Lamentations 2:18-19

*Their heart cried out to the Lord, "O wall of the daughter of Zion, let tears run down like a river day and night; give yourself no relief; give your eyes no rest. Arise, cry out in the night, at the beginning of the watches; pour out your heart like water before the face of the Lord. Lift your hands toward Him for the life of your young children, who faint from hunger at the head of every street."*

## I Timothy 2:1

*Therefore I exhort first of all that supplications, prayers, intercessions, and giving of thanks be made for all men.*

## Isaiah 59:13-16

*In transgressing and lying against the LORD, and departing from our God, speaking oppression and revolt, conceiving and uttering from the heart words of falsehood. Justice is turned back, and righteousness stands afar off; for truth is fallen in the street, and equity cannot enter. So truth fails, and he who departs from evil makes himself a prey. Then the LORD saw it, and it displeased Him that there was no justice. He saw that there was no man, and wondered that there was no intercessor; therefore His own arm brought salvation for Him; and His own righteousness, it sustained Him.*

## Luke 2:36-37

*Now there was one, Anna, a prophetess, the daughter of Phanuel, of the tribe of Asher. She was of a great age, and had lived with a husband seven years from her virginity; and this woman was a widow of about eighty-four years, who did not depart from the temple, but served God with fastings and prayers night and day.*

## Revelation 8:3-4

*Then another angel, having a golden censer, came and stood at the altar. He was given much incense, that he should offer it with the prayers of all the saints upon the golden altar which was before the throne. And the smoke of the incense, with the prayers of the saints, ascended before God from the angel's hand.*

## Romans 8:26

*Likewise the Spirit also helps in our weaknesses. For we do not know what we should pray for as we ought, but the Spirit Himself makes intercession for us with groanings which cannot be uttered.*

## John 15:16

*You did not choose Me, but I chose you and appointed you that you should go and bear fruit, and that your fruit should remain, that whatever you ask the Father in My name He may give you.*

## Acts 4:31

*And when they had prayed, the place where they were assembled together was shaken; and they were all filled with the Holy Spirit, and they spoke the word of God with boldness.*

## Revelation 5:8

*Now when He had taken the scroll, the four living creatures and the twenty-four elders fell down before the Lamb, each having a harp, and golden bowls full of incense, which are the prayers of the saints.*

# Day Ten

## *New Spiritual Power by Being Cleansed*

Lord, I desire a new dimension in my life for new spiritual power. I desire to make room for more of You, Lord, by renewing the old, taking away the impure. Cleanse me, Lord, from secret faults. Wash me thoroughly from my iniquity. Purge me and purify my heart, O Lord. Come visit every room of my house. Enter and take control. It all belongs to You! Fill these rooms with a new presence, a new word, a new song. Fill me with Your treasures, O Lord. Create in me a clean heart and renew a right spirit within me. Come Refiner's Fire and burn away all the dross. Come Holy Spirit and bring to my mind anything and everything that I've done knowingly or unknowingly and forgive me. Cleanse me by the power of the blood of Jesus. Create in me a new spiritual momentum that flows freely from a cleansed life.

## I John 1:7-9

*But if we walk in the light as He is in the light, we have fellowship with one another, and the blood of Jesus Christ His Son cleanses us from all sin. If we say that we have no sin, we deceive ourselves, and the truth is not in us. If we confess our sins, He is faithful and just to forgive us our sins and to cleanse us from all unrighteousness.*

## Hebrews 9:22-28

*And according to the law almost all things are purified with blood, and without shedding of blood there is no remission. Therefore it was necessary that the copies of the things in the heavens should be purified with these, but the heavenly things themselves with better sacrifices than these. For Christ has not entered the holy places made with hands, which are copies of the true, but into heaven itself, now to appear in the presence of God for us; not that He should offer Himself often, as the high priest enters the Most Holy Place every year with blood of another— He then would have had to suffer often since the foundation of the world; but now, once at the end of the ages, He has appeared to put away sin by the sacrifice of Himself. And as it is appointed for men to die once, but after this the judgment, so Christ was offered once to bear the sins of many. To those who eagerly wait for Him He will appear a second time, apart from sin, for salvation.*

## Ephesians 1:7

*In Him we have redemption through His blood, the forgiveness of sins, according to the riches of His grace.*

## Romans 5:9

*Much more then, having now been justified by His blood, we shall be saved from wrath through Him.*

## Isaiah 4:2-6

*In that day the Branch of the LORD shall be beautiful and glorious; and the fruit of the earth shall be excellent and appealing for those of Israel who have escaped. And it shall come to pass that he who is left in Zion and remains in Jerusalem will be called holy—everyone who is recorded among the living in Jerusalem. When the Lord has washed away the filth of the daughters of Zion, and purged the blood of Jerusalem from her midst, by the spirit of judgment and by the spirit* of burning, then the LORD will create above every dwelling place of Mount Zion, and above her assemblies, a cloud and smoke by day and the shining of a flaming fire by night. For over all the glory there will be a covering.  And there will be a tabernacle for shade in the daytime from the heat, for a place of refuge, and for a shelter from storm and rain.

## Psalms 51:2, 7

*Wash me thoroughly from my iniquity, and cleanse me from my sin. Purge me with hyssop, and I shall be clean; wash me, and I shall be whiter than snow.*

## Isaiah 1:16

*Wash yourselves, make yourselves clean; put away the evil of your doings from before My eyes. Cease to do evil.*

## 2 Corinthians 7:1

*Therefore, having these promises, beloved, let us cleanse ourselves from all filthiness of the flesh and spirit, perfecting holiness in the fear of God.*

## James 4:8

*Draw near to God and He will draw near to you. Cleanse your hands, you sinners; and purify your hearts, you double-minded.*

## Revelation 1:5

*And from Jesus Christ, the faithful witness, the firstborn from the dead, and the ruler over the kings of the earth. To Him who loved us and washed us from our sins in His own blood.*

## Psalms 19:12

*Who can understand his errors? Cleanse me from secret faults.*

## Psalms 66:18

*If I regard iniquity in my heart, the Lord will not hear.*

## Nehemiah 13:9

*Then I commanded them to cleanse the rooms; and I brought back into them the articles of the house of God, with the grain offering and the frankincense.*

## Proverbs 24:4

*By knowledge the rooms are filled with all precious and pleasant riches.*

# Day Eleven

## *New Spiritual Power to Focus on God*

God, come visit me and reveal Yourself to me by and through the Holy Spirit and the word of God. Reveal Your ways and Your truth. Breathe into me Your very thoughts and words for You desire to speak with me and I desire to hear Your voice. Unveil Your purposes and teach me Your ways. Lord, today I set my heart and soul to seek You and know You and You have promised that You will be found by those who seek You with all their heart. You desire, O Lord, to be actively involved with my life. You are never indifferent, cold or disinterested. You are eager to be with me and to guide me, protect

me, love me, forgive me. Today, I focus on
You and ask for new spiritual momentum in
my prayer life.

## Psalm 18:2

*The LORD is my rock and my fortress and my deliverer; My God, my strength, in whom I will trust; My shield and the horn of my salvation, my stronghold.*

## Jeremiah 9:23-24

*Thus says the LORD: "Let not the wise man glory in his wisdom, let not the mighty man glory in his might, nor let the rich man glory in his riches; but let him who glories glory in this, that he understands and knows Me, that I am the LORD, exercising lovingkindness, judgment, and righteousness in the earth. For in these I delight," says the LORD.*

## Hosea 6:6

*For I desire mercy and not sacrifice, and the knowledge of God more than burnt offerings.*

## Jeremiah 32:17-19

*Ah, Lord GOD! Behold, You have made the heavens and the earth by Your great power and outstretched arm. There is nothing too hard for You. You show lovingkindness to thou-*

sands, and repay the iniquity of the fathers into the bosom of their children after them—the Great, the Mighty God, whose name is the LORD of hosts. You are great in counsel and mighty in work, for Your eyes are open to all the ways of the sons of men, to give everyone according to his ways and according to the fruit of his doings.

## Psalm 78:38-39

But He, being full of compassion, forgave their iniquity, and did not destroy them. Yes, many a time He turned His anger away, and did not stir up all His wrath; for He remembered that they were but flesh, a breath that passes away and does not come again.

## Psalm 86:15

But You, O Lord, are a God full of compassion, and gracious, longsuffering and abundant in mercy and truth.

## I Kings 8:56

"Blessed be the LORD, who has given rest to His people Israel, according to all that He promised. There has not failed one *word of all His good promise, which He promised through His servant Moses."*

## Lamentations 3:21-23

*This I recall to my mind, therefore I have hope. Through the LORD's mercies we are not consumed, because His compassions fail not. They are new every morning; great is Your faithfulness.*

## Hebrews 12:2

*Looking unto Jesus, the author and finisher of our faith, who for the joy that was set before Him endured the cross, despising the shame, and has sat down at the right hand of the throne of God.*

## Hebrews 10:23

*Let us hold fast the confession of our hope without wavering, for He who promised is faithful.*

## Isaiah 46:9-10

*Remember the former things of old, for I am God, and there* is no other; I am God, and there is none like Me, declaring the end from the beginning, and from ancient times things that are not yet done, saying, 'My counsel shall stand, and I will do all My pleasure'.

## Job 11:7

"Can you fathom the mysteries of God? Can you probe the limits of the Almighty?

## Psalms 14:2

The LORD looks down from heaven upon the children of men, to see if there are any who understand, who seek God.

## 1 Chronicles 22:19

Now set your heart and your soul to seek the LORD your God. Therefore arise and build the sanctuary of the LORD God, to bring the ark of the covenant of the LORD and the holy articles of God into the house that is to be built for the name of the LORD.

# Day Twelve

## *New Spiritual Power to Break Through*

In the mighty name of Jesus, I pray with great faith that the new doors You have for my life will open. I will break through to new life opportunities and new anointing, by the power of the Holy Spirit. I will remove all longstanding obstacles through faith, prayer, and fasting. By faith, I stretch toward the new challenges You have set before me. I will not draw back. I will not lose heart. By faith, I will destroy any obstacle that hinders progress and I will advance beyond all previous limitations. I will not quit, give in, or give up. I will not retreat, back off, or step down. I will not shift into neutral, take a break, or do nothing. But by God's grace, I will break through and move ahead with supernatural strength.

### Micah 2:13

*The one who breaks open will come up before them; they will break out, pass through the gate, and go out by it; their king will pass before them, with the LORD at their head.*

### Psalms 24:7-10

*Lift up your heads, O you gates! And be lifted up, you everlasting doors! And the King of glory shall come in. Who is this King of glory? The LORD strong and mighty, the LORD mighty in battle. Lift up your heads, O you gates! Lift up, you everlasting doors! And the King of glory shall come in. Who is this King of glory? The LORD of hosts, He is the King of glory.*

### Matthew 12:29

*Or how can one enter a strong man's house and plunder his goods, unless he first binds the strong man? And then he will plunder his house.*

## Genesis 22:17

*Blessing I will bless you, and multiplying I will multiply your descendants as the stars of the heaven and as the sand which is on the seashore; and your descendants shall possess the gate of their enemies.*

## Isaiah 64:1-2

*Oh, that You would rend the heavens! That You would come down! That the mountains might shake at Your presence. As fire burns brushwood, as fire causes water to boil to make Your name known to Your adversaries that the nations may tremble at Your presence!*

## Matthew 12:2

*And when the Pharisees saw it, they said to Him, "Look, Your disciples are doing what is not lawful to do on the Sabbath!"*

## Joshua 8:18

*Then the LORD said to Joshua, "Stretch out the spear that is in your hand toward Ai, for I will give it into your hand." And Joshua stretched out the spear that was in his hand toward the city.*

## Joshua 8:26

*For Joshua did not draw back his hand, with which he stretched out the spear, until he had utterly destroyed all the inhabitants of Ai.*

## Isaiah 58:8

*Then your light shall break forth like the morning, Your healing shall spring forth speedily, and your righteousness shall go before you; the glory of the LORD shall be your rear guard.*

## Philippians 3:12-14

*Not that I have already attained, or am already perfected; but I press on, that I may lay hold of that for which Christ Jesus has also laid hold of me. Brethren, I do not count myself to have apprehended; but one thing I do, forgetting those things which are behind and reaching forward to those things which are ahead, I press toward the goal for the prize of the upward call of God in Christ Jesus.*

# Day Thirteen

## *New Spiritual Power to Reach the Lost*

Lord, I pray for a new understanding of hell and a new commitment to reaching people with the Gospel. Lord, make me a willing witness. Give me divine appointments with people You have already prepared to hear the gospel. As You work through me by the Holy Spirit, give me divinely arranged meetings to touch people. Lord, give me eyes to see the multitudes of people who have multiplied needs, multitudes of people who are in desperate places, people who are spiritually confused or spiritually lost. Lord, use my life to touch people today and every day. Lord, I pray for the lost, the prodigals, the futile and fools, the deceived, the bound, the depraved minded, and those trapped in any way by the devil. Release them and let them go in Jesus name. Create in me a new intensity that will thrust me in the lives of these people.

## Isaiah 43:5-6

*Fear not, for I am with you; I will bring your descendants from the east, and gather you from the west; I will say to the north, 'Give them up!' and to the south, 'Do not keep them back!' Bring My sons from afar and My daughters from the ends of the earth.*

## Mark 2:17

*When Jesus heard it, He said to them, "Those who are well have no need of a physician, but those who are sick. I did not come to call the righteous, but sinners, to repentance."*

## Acts 17:4-5

*And some of them were persuaded; and a great multitude of the devout Greeks, and not a few of the leading women, joined Paul and Silas. But the Jews who were not persuaded, becoming envious, took some of the evil men from the marketplace, and gathering a mob, set all the city in an uproar and attacked the house of Jason, and sought to bring them out to the people.*

## Matthew 9:35-37

*Then Jesus went about all the cities and villages, teaching in their synagogues, preaching the gospel of the kingdom, and healing every sickness and every disease among the people. But when He saw the multitudes, He was moved with compassion for them, because they were weary and scattered, like sheep having no shepherd. Then He said to His disciples, "The harvest truly is plentiful, but the laborers are few."*

## 2 Corinthians 4:4-5

*Whose minds the god of this age has blinded, who do not believe, lest the light of the gospel of the glory of Christ, who is the image of God, should shine on them. For we do not preach ourselves, but Christ Jesus the Lord, and ourselves your bondservants for Jesus' sake.*

## Acts 4:29-31

*Now, Lord, look on their threats, and grant to Your servants that with all boldness they may speak Your word, by stretching out Your hand to heal, and that signs and wonders may be done through the name of Your holy Servant Jesus." And when they had prayed, the place where they were assembled*

together was shaken; and they were all filled with the Holy
Spirit, and they spoke the word of God with boldness.

## Isaiah 61:1

"The Spirit of the Lord GOD is upon Me, because the LORD has
anointed Me to preach good tidings to the poor; He has sent
Me to heal the brokenhearted, to proclaim liberty to the captives, and the opening of the prison to those who are bound."

## Mathew 18:18

Assuredly, I say to you, whatever you bind on earth will be
bound in heaven, and whatever you loose on earth will be
loosed in heaven.

## Isaiah 58:6

Is this not the fast that I have chosen: to loose the bonds of
wickedness, to undo the heavy burdens, to let the oppressed
go free, and that you break every yoke?

## Ephesians 6:18

*Praying always with all prayer and supplication in the Spirit, being watchful to this end with all perseverance and supplication for all the saints.*

## Revelation 20:12-15

*And I saw the dead, small and great, standing before God, and books were opened. And another book was opened, which is the Book of Life. And the dead were judged according to their works, by the things which were written in the books. The sea gave up the dead who were in it, and Death and Hades delivered up the dead who were in them. And they were judged, each one according to his works. Then Death and Hades were cast into the lake of fire. This is the second death. And anyone not found written in the Book of Life was cast into the lake of fire.*

## Matthew 13:40-42

*Therefore as the tares are gathered and burned in the fire, so it will be at the end of this age. The Son of Man will send out His angels, and they will gather out of His kingdom all things that offend, and those who practice lawlessness, and* will cast them into the furnace of fire. There will be wailing and gnashing of teeth.

## Revelation 14:11

And the smoke of their torment ascends forever and ever; and they have no rest day or night, who worship the beast and his image, and whoever receives the mark of his name.

# Day Fourteen

## *New Spiritual Power to Be Specific*

Lord, I take this time to turn my focus away from myself and turn it to You. Deliver me from the distractions, problems, and details of living in this world. Let me remember that You are God! You are the Creator of all things and You have the power to grant my request. Lord, give me the faith to be specific, asking for those things I see and for those things I can't see. Give me an eternal perspective on life and the things I pray for. Holy Spirit, come and fill my mind with God thoughts! Reveal to me what I should pray for and how I should pray. Give me faith to be specific and to hit the target I aim for in my prayers.

## Luke 11:11-13

*If a son asks for bread from any father among you, will he give him a stone? Or if he asks for a fish, will he give him a serpent instead of a fish? Or if he asks for an egg, will he offer him a scorpion? If you then, being evil, know how to give good gifts to your children, how much more will your heavenly Father give the Holy Spirit to those who ask Him!*

## James 1:6-7

*But let him ask in faith, with no doubting, for he who doubts is like a wave of the sea driven and tossed by the wind. For let not that man suppose that he will receive anything from the Lord.*

## John 15:7

*If you abide in Me, and My words abide in you, you will ask what you desire, and it shall be done for you.*

## Matthew 7:7-8

Ask, and it will be given to you; seek, and you will find; knock, and it will be opened to you. For everyone who asks receives, and he who seeks finds, and to him who knocks it will be opened.

## Matthew 21:22

And whatever things you ask in prayer, believing, you will receive.

## 1 John 5:14-15

Now this is the confidence that we have in Him, that if we ask anything according to His will, He hears us. And if we know that He hears us, whatever we ask, we know that we have the petitions that we have asked of Him.

## Isaiah 55:8-9

"For My thoughts are not your thoughts, nor are your ways My ways," says the LORD. "For as the heavens are higher than the earth, so are My ways higher than your ways, and My thoughts than your thoughts."

## Luke 9:41

*Then Jesus answered and said, "O faithless and perverse generation, how long shall I be with you and bear with you? Bring your son here."*

## Jeremiah 33:3

*Call to Me, and I will answer you, and show you great and mighty things, which you do not know!*

## Romans 8:26-27

*Likewise the Spirit also helps in our weaknesses. For we do not know what we should pray for as we ought, but the Spirit Himself makes intercession for us with groanings which cannot be uttered. Now He who searches the hearts knows what the mind of the Spirit is, because He makes intercession for the saints according to the will of God.*

# Day Fifteen

## *Fresh Anointing on My Personal Vision*

Lord Jesus, give me the vision I should have for my life. Give me the faith and the courage to dream big! Expand my thinking with Your thoughts. Lord, place some vision seeds into my life, water them, and give them growth to full maturity. Lord, lead me into those paths You have ordained for my life. Give me the relationships that will help create vision momentum in my life. Keep me from associating with faithless, unbelieving, small-minded and small-spirited people. Surround my life with faith people, those with a no-limitation vision or capacity. Lord Jesus, let me dream those dreams made by Your workings. Let me have the dedication needed to pay for the price for those dreams to be fulfilled. Enlarge my vision today. Anoint me with a fresh new hope for the future. I surrender my life to Your hands, knowing You have predestined the best for my life.

## Acts 16:9-10

And a vision appeared to Paul in the night. A man of Macedonia stood and pleaded with him, saying, "Come over to Macedonia and help us." Now after he had seen the vision, immediately we sought to go to Macedonia, concluding that the Lord had called us to preach the gospel to them."

## Acts 26:19

Therefore, King Agrippa, I was not disobedient to the heavenly vision.

## 1 Timothy 1:18-19

This charge I commit to you, son Timothy, according to the prophecies previously made concerning you, that by them you may wage the good warfare, having faith and a good conscience, which some having rejected, concerning the faith have suffered shipwreck.

## 2 Chronicles 1:7

On that night God appeared to Solomon, and said to him, "Ask! What shall I give you?"

## Ezekiel 1:1

*In the thirtieth year, in the fourth month on the fifth day, while I was among the exiles by the Kebar River, the heavens were opened and I saw visions of God.*

## I Corinthians 14:14-15

*For if I pray in a tongue, my spirit prays, but my understanding is unfruitful. What is the conclusion then? I will pray with the spirit, and I will also pray with the understanding. I will sing with the spirit, and I will also sing with the understanding.*

## I Samuel 3:10

*Now the LORD came and stood and called as at other times, "Samuel! Samuel!" And Samuel answered, "Speak, for Your servant hears."*

## Ephesians 1:17-18

*That the God of our Lord Jesus Christ, the Father of glory, may give to you the spirit of wisdom and revelation in the knowledge of Him, the eyes of your understanding being en-*

lightened; that you may know what is the hope of His calling, what are the riches of the glory of His inheritance in the saints.

## James 3:4

Look also at ships: although they are so large and are driven by fierce winds, they are turned by a very small rudder wherever the pilot desires.

## 2 Timothy 4:7

I have fought the good fight, I have finished the race, I have kept the faith.

# Day Sixteen

## *Fresh Anointing on My Church Leadership*

Lord, I pray a fresh anointing upon all our church leaders. Anoint them with a spirit of tenacity and resolve. Strengthen them so they will hold to the vision with steadfast determination. Anoint every leader with new, fresh God thoughts that are above and beyond the thoughts or ideas of men. Anoint every leader with the power of the Holy Spirit to do all they are called to do. Refresh them today in body, soul and spirit. Send the Holy Spirit today to lift them up and encourage them. Lord anoint them with a new mantle of leadership to accomplish Your work. Protect them and build a hedge around their marriages, their families, their health and their spiritual well-being. Let them receive from You a strong heart to finish the work with faith and integrity.

## 2 Corinthians 10:8

*For even if I should boast somewhat more about our authority, which the Lord gave us for edification and not for your destruction, I shall not be ashamed.*

## 1 Peter 1:15-17

*But as He who called you is holy, you also be holy in all your conduct, because it is written, "Be holy, for I am holy." And if you call on the Father, who without partiality judges according to each one's work, conduct yourselves throughout the time of your stay here in fear.*

## Jeremiah 29:11-12

*For I know the thoughts that I think toward you, says the LORD, thoughts of peace and not of evil, to give you a future and a hope. Then you will call upon Me and go and pray to Me, and I will listen to you.*

## Isaiah 62:6-7

*I have set watchmen on your walls, O Jerusalem; they shall never hold their peace day or night. You who make mention of the LORD, do not keep silent, and give Him no rest till He establishes and till He makes Jerusalem a praise in the earth.*

## Joel 1:13-14

*Gird yourselves and lament, you priests; wail, you who minister before the altar; come, lie all night in sackcloth, you who minister to my God; for the grain offering and the drink offering are withheld from the house of your God. Consecrate a fast, call a sacred assembly; gather the elders and all the inhabitants of the land into the house of the LORD your God, and cry out to the LORD.*

## Numbers 11:16-17

*So the LORD said to Moses: "Gather to Me seventy men of the elders of Israel, whom you know to be the elders of the people and officers over them; bring them to the tabernacle of meeting, that they may stand there with you. Then I will come down and talk with you there. I will take of the Spirit* that is upon you and will put the same upon them; and they shall bear the burden of the people with you, that you may not bear it yourself alone."

## Ecclesiastes 4:9-12

Two are better than one, because they have a good reward for their labor. For if they fall, one will lift up his companion. But woe to him who is alone when he falls, for he has no one to help him up. Again, if two lie down together, they will keep warm; but how can one be warm alone? Though one may be overpowered by another, two can withstand him. And a threefold cord is not quickly broken.

## Proverbs 31:23

Her husband is known in the gates, when he sits among the elders of the land.

## I Corinthians 2:4-5, 9-10

And my speech and my preaching were not with persuasive words of human wisdom, but in demonstration of the Spirit and of power, that your faith should not be in the wisdom of *men but in the power of God. But as it is written: "Eye has not seen, nor ear heard, nor have entered into the heart of man the things which God has prepared for those who love Him." But God has revealed them to us through His Spirit. For the Spirit searches all things, yes, the deep things of God.*

## I Kings 2:13-15

*Now Adonijah the son of Haggith came to Bathsheba the mother of Solomon. So she said, "Do you come peaceably?" And he said, "Peaceably." Moreover he said, "I have something to say to you." And she said, "Say it." Then he said, "You know that the kingdom was mine, and all Israel had set their expectations on me, that I should reign. However, the kingdom has been turned over, and has become my brother's; for it was his from the LORD."*

# Day Seventeen

## *Fresh Anointing on My Church Vision*

Lord, I pray a fresh anointing upon the vision You have given my church. Do not let us shrink back from the greatness of Your vision for the church. Let us see the vision clearly and progress toward fulfilling that vision continuously with faith and persistence. Give me a heart to support the vision in every way. Give me the strength to participate with all my heart in the fulfillment of our vision. Let the leaders of the vision see and feel my heart and faith for the vision. Lord, give me courage and faith as we face the challenges and take risks in pursuing the vision. Lord, I believe You brought me to this church to enlarge my vision and to enlarge my spiritual capacity. Thank you Lord for a church with a big vision and the faith to go after it. Give me the passion, motivation, and energy to help accomplish this vision.

## Zechariah 4:1-2

*Now the angel who talked with me came back and wakened me, as a man who is wakened out of his sleep. And he said to me, "What do you see?" So I said, "I am looking, and there is a lampstand of solid gold with a bowl on top of it, and on the stand seven lamps with seven pipes to the seven lamps."*

## Isaiah 54:1-3

*"Sing, O barren, you who have not borne! Break forth into singing, and cry aloud, you who have not labored with child! For more are the children of the desolate than the children of the married woman," says the LORD. "Enlarge the place of your tent, and let them stretch out the curtains of your dwellings; do not spare; lengthen your cords, and strengthen your stakes. For you shall expand to the right and to the left, and your descendants will inherit the nations, and make the desolate cities inhabited."*

## Habakkuk 2:1-3

*I will stand my watch and set myself on the rampart, and watch to see what He will say to me, and what I will answer when I am corrected. Then the LORD answered me and said:*

*"Write the vision and make it plain on tablets, that he may run who reads it. For the vision is yet for an appointed time; but at the end it will speak, and it will not lie. Though it tarries, wait for it; because it will surely come, it will not tarry.*

## Daniel 9:19

*O Lord, hear! O Lord, forgive! O Lord, listen and act! Do not delay for Your own sake, my God, for Your city and Your people are called by Your name.*

## Joshua 17:14-17

*Then the children of Joseph spoke to Joshua, saying, "Why have you given us only one lot and one share to inherit, since we are a great people, inasmuch as the LORD has blessed us until now?" So Joshua answered them, "If you are a great people, then go up to the forest country and clear a place for yourself there in the land of the Perizzites and the giants, since the mountains of Ephraim are too confined for you." But the children of Joseph said, "The mountain country is not enough for us; and all the Canaanites who dwell in the land of the valley have chariots of iron, both those who are of Beth Shean and its towns and those who are of the Val-*

ley of Jezreel." And Joshua spoke to the house of Joseph—to Ephraim and Manasseh—saying, "You are a great people and have great power; you shall not have only one lot but the mountain country shall be yours. Although it is wooded, you shall cut it down, and its farthest extent shall be yours; for you shall drive out the Canaanites, though they have iron chariots and are strong."

## Jonah 3:7-10

And he caused it to be proclaimed and published throughout Nineveh by the decree of the king and his nobles, saying, let neither man nor beast, herd nor flock, taste anything; do not let them eat, or drink water. But let man and beast be covered with sackcloth, and cry mightily to God; yes, let every one turn from his evil way and from the violence that is in his hands. Who can tell if God will turn and relent, and turn away from His fierce anger, so that we may not perish? Then God saw their works, that they turned from their evil way; and God relented from the disaster that He had said He would bring upon them, and He did not do it.

### Genesis 13:17

*Arise, walk in the land through its length and its width, for I give it to you.*

### 2 Chronicles 2:5

*And the temple which I build will be great, for our God is greater than all gods.*

### Acts 4:33

*And with great power the apostles gave witness to the resurrection of the Lord Jesus. And great grace was upon them all.*

# Day Eighteen

## *Fresh Anointing on My Prayer and Worship*

Lord, I pray today for a fresh anointing of the Holy Spirit upon the prayer and worship of my church. Lord, help us to sustain a prayer atmosphere through intercessory prayer in which every believer faithfully participates in fervent prayer at all times, for all things. Release the supernatural powers of God in an obvious and awesome manner. Help me, Lord, to add to our prayer spirit and prayer atmosphere by being a prayer person. Lord, anoint our worship with a fresh touch of the Holy Spirit. Lord, I will praise You with my whole heart. I will sing praise to Your name, O Most High! I will exalt You with my words and with the lifting of my hands. For

You, Lord, are holy and You inhabit the praises of Your people. Come today and invade my life with Your presence. Come invade our worship times at my church. Saturate Your people with Your presence.

### Acts 4:31

*And when they had prayed, the place where they were assembled together was shaken; and they were all filled with the Holy Spirit, and they spoke the word of God with boldness.*

### Ephesians 6:18

*Praying always with all prayer and supplication in the Spirit, being watchful to this end with all perseverance and supplication for all the saints.*

### Acts 1:14

*These all continued with one accord in prayer and supplication, with the women and Mary the mother of Jesus, and with His brothers.*

### Acts 2:42

*And they continued steadfastly in the apostles' doctrine and fellowship, in the breaking of bread, and in prayers.*

## Romans 8:26-27

*Likewise the Spirit also helps in our weaknesses. For we do not know what we should pray for as we ought, but the Spirit Himself makes intercession for us with groanings which cannot be uttered. Now He who searches the hearts knows what the mind of the Spirit is, because He makes intercession for the saints according to the will of God.*

## Hebrews 5:7

*Who, in the days of His flesh, when He had offered up prayers and supplications, with vehement cries and tears to Him who was able to save Him from death, and was heard because of His godly fear.*

## Psalms 22:3

*But You are holy, enthroned in the praises of Israel.*

## Psalms 141:2

*Let my prayer be set before You as incense, the lifting up of my hands as the evening sacrifice.*

## Revelation 5:8

*Now when He had taken the scroll, the four living creatures and the twenty-four elders fell down before the Lamb, each having a harp, and golden bowls full of incense, which are the prayers of the saints.*

## Revelation 8:3-5

*Then another angel, having a golden censer, came and stood at the altar. He was given much incense, that he should offer it with the prayers of all the saints upon the golden altar which was before the throne. And the smoke of the incense, with the prayers of the saints, ascended before God from the angel's hand. Then the angel took the censer, filled it with fire from the altar, and threw it to the earth. And there were noises, thunderings, lightnings, and an earthquake.*

## Isaiah 61:1-3

*"The Spirit of the Lord GOD is upon Me, because the LORD has anointed Me to preach good tidings to the poor; He has sent Me to heal the brokenhearted, to proclaim liberty to the captives, and the opening of the prison to those who are bound; to proclaim the acceptable year of the LORD, and the day of*

vengeance of our God; to comfort all who mourn, to console those who mourn in Zion, to give them beauty for ashes, the oil of joy for mourning, the garment of praise for the spirit of heaviness; that they may be called trees of righteousness, the planting of the LORD, that He may be glorified."

## I Timothy 2:1

Therefore I exhort first of all that supplications, prayers, intercessions, and giving of thanks be made for all men.

## Psalms 5:7

But as for me, I will come into Your house in the multitude of Your mercy; in fear of You I will worship toward Your holy temple.

## Psalms 9:1

I will praise You, O LORD, with my whole heart; I will tell of all Your marvelous works.

## I Peter 2:5

You also, as living stones, are being built up a spiritual house, a holy priesthood, to offer up spiritual sacrifices acceptable to God through Jesus Christ.

## Psalms 111:1

*Praise the LORD! I will praise the LORD with my whole heart, in the assembly of the upright and in the congregation.*

# Day Nineteen

## *Fresh Anointing on My World Vision*

Lord, give me a heart and faith to pray for the nations of the world to be reached with the gospel of Christ. Give me a God-sized vision of the world. Make me a world thinker, a world prayer, a world giver. Lord, I claim the nations as my inheritance and the ends of the earth as my possession. Lord, I pray that every nation will receive church planting and church leadership, training missionaries who will see churches planted in every city, village, town, and province of every nation in the world. For the earth – every tongue, tribe, and people – is the Lord's and all its fullness. The world and all those who dwell therein belong to the You, O God. Lord, remove the veil of unbelief that is stretched over many nations. Destroy the dark covering over the people and the veil that is spread over the nations. Lord, I see these people coming to Christ. I see the gospel penetrating the culture. I see a great multitude that no one can number of all nations, tribes, people, and tongues standing before the throne of God. Thank you, Lord, for moving in all the world and making me a world vision person.

## Revelation 7:9-10

*After these things I looked, and behold, a great multitude which no one could number, of all nations, tribes, peoples, and tongues, standing before the throne and before the Lamb, clothed with white robes, with palm branches in their hands, and crying out with a loud voice, saying, "Salvation belongs to our God who sits on the throne, and to the Lamb!"*

## John 3:16

*For God so loved the world that He gave His only begotten Son, that whoever believes in Him should not perish but have everlasting life.*

## John 1:29

*The next day John saw Jesus coming toward him, and said, "Behold! The Lamb of God who takes away the sin of the world!*

## Isaiah 60:1

*Arise, shine; for your light has come! and the glory of the LORD is risen upon you.*

## Acts 1:8

*But you shall receive power when the Holy Spirit has come upon you; and you shall be witnesses to Me in Jerusalem, and in all Judea and Samaria, and to the end of the earth.*

## Matthew 28:16-20

*Then the eleven disciples went away into Galilee, to the mountain which Jesus had appointed for them. When they saw Him, they worshiped Him; but some doubted. And Jesus came and spoke to them, saying, "All authority has been given to Me in heaven and on earth. Go therefore and make disciples of all the nations, baptizing them in the name of the Father and of the Son and of the Holy Spirit, teaching them to observe all things that I have commanded you; and lo, I am with you always, even to the end of the age."*

## Acts 13:1-3

*Now in the church that was at Antioch there were certain prophets and teachers: Barnabas, Simeon who was called Niger, Lucius of Cyrene, Manaen who had been brought up with Herod the tetrarch, and Saul. As they ministered to the Lord and fasted, the Holy Spirit said, "Now separate to Me*

Barnabas and Saul for the work to which I have called them."
Then, having fasted and prayed, and laid hands on them,
they sent them away.

### Psalms 24:1

The earth is the LORD's, and all its fullness, the world and
those who dwell therein.

### Revelation 14:6

Then I saw another angel flying in the midst of heaven, having the everlasting gospel to preach to those who dwell on
the earth—to every nation, tribe, tongue, and people.

### Habakkuk 2:14

For the earth will be filled with the knowledge of the glory of
the LORD, as the waters cover the sea.

### Genesis 18:18

Since Abraham shall surely become a great and mighty nation, and all the nations of the earth shall be blessed in him?

## Psalms 2:8

*Ask of Me, and I will give You the nations for Your inheritance, and the ends of the earth for Your possession.*

## Isaiah 25:6-7

*And in this mountain the LORD of hosts will make for all people a feast of choice pieces, a feast of wines on the lees, of fat things full of marrow, of well-refined wines on the lees. And He will destroy on this mountain the surface of the covering cast over all people, and the veil that is spread over all nations.*

## 2 Corinthians 5:19

*That is, that God was in Christ reconciling the world to Himself, not imputing their trespasses to them, and has committed to us the word of reconciliation.*

## Matthew 24:14

*And this gospel of the kingdom will be preached in all the world as a witness to all the nations, and then the end will come.*

## Habakkuk 1:5

*Look among the nations and watch— Be utterly astounded! For I will work a work in your days which you would not believe, though it were told you.*

# Day Twenty

## *Fresh Anointing on My Faith for Miracles*

Lord, I believe that You are the God of miracles. Give me a heart of expectation and an attitude of faith that says God can, God is able, God is willing. Teach me, Lord, to develop a belief system that believes nothing is impossible with God. Lord, let Your ordained miracles be in me, around me, and through me. Lord, I believe You have miracles prepared for me today and every day, miraculous and life-changing miracles. A miracle is on its way to intercept me right now. I'm looking for these miracles, believing, reaching, praying, and expecting. Lord, I see miracles coming my way in my finances, my relationships, my physical body, my job, my family, my life.

Lord, let me receive things beyond my seeing, things beyond my hearing, things beyond my imagining, things You have prepared for me. New visions, new dreams, new passions, new miracles are coming my way. Lord, I accept Your supernatural working in my life and my future. Let the miracles begin!

### I Corinthians 2:9-10

*But as it is written: "Eye has not seen, nor ear heard, nor have entered into the heart of man the things which God has prepared for those who love Him." But God has revealed them to us through His Spirit. For the Spirit searches all things, yes, the deep things of God.*

### Hebrews 13:8

*Jesus Christ is the same yesterday, today, and forever.*

### Luke 7:16

*Then fear came upon all, and they glorified God, saying, "A great prophet has risen up among us"; and, "God has visited His people."*

### Matthew 8:2-3

*And behold, a leper came and worshiped Him, saying, "Lord, if You are willing, You can make me clean." Then Jesus put out His hand and touched him, saying, "I am willing; be cleansed." Immediately his leprosy was cleansed.*

## Matthew 16:16-18

*Simon Peter answered and said, "You are the Christ, the Son of the living God."*

*Jesus answered and said to him, "Blessed are you, Simon Bar-Jonah, for flesh and blood has not revealed this to you, but My Father who is in heaven. And I also say to you that you are Peter, and on this rock I will build My church, and the gates of Hades shall not prevail against it."*

## Matthew 15:25-28

*Then she came and worshiped Him, saying, "Lord, help me!" But He answered and said, "It is not good to take the children's bread and throw it to the little dogs." And she said, "Yes, Lord, yet even the little dogs eat the crumbs which fall from their masters' table." Then Jesus answered and said to her, "O woman, great is your faith! Let it be to you as you desire." And her daughter was healed from that very hour.*

## John 5:1-4

*After this there was a feast of the Jews, and Jesus went up to Jerusalem. Now there is in Jerusalem by the Sheep Gate a pool, which is called in Hebrew, Bethesda, having five porches. In these lay a great multitude of sick people, blind, lame, paralyzed, waiting for the moving of the water. For an angel went down at a certain time into the pool and stirred up the water; then whoever stepped in first, after the stirring of the water, was made well of whatever disease he had.*

## James 5:15

*And the prayer of faith will save the sick, and the Lord will raise him up. And if he has committed sins, he will be forgiven.*

## Judges 6:13

*Gideon said to Him, "O my lord, if the LORD is with us, why then has all this happened to us? And where are all His miracles which our fathers told us about, saying, 'Did not the LORD bring us up from Egypt?' But now the LORD has forsaken us and delivered us into the hands of the Midianites."*

## Acts 6:8

*And Stephen, full of faith and power, did great wonders and signs among the people.*

## Acts 14:3, 8-10

*Therefore they stayed there a long time, speaking boldly in the Lord, who was bearing witness to the word of His grace, granting signs and wonders to be done by their hands. And in Lystra a certain man without strength in his feet was sitting, a cripple from his mother's womb, who had never walked. This man heard Paul speaking. Paul, observing him intently and seeing that he had faith to be healed, said with a loud voice, "Stand up straight on your feet!" And he leaped and walked.*

# Day Twenty-One

## *Fresh Anointing on My Personal Life*

Father God, I receive this day a new, fresh, powerful anointing upon my life, a yoke-breaking anointing, a prayer-breakthrough anointing. Father God, let Your Holy Spirit come upon me mightily today, upon my body, soul and spirit, upon my mind, will and emotions. Anoint my life with Holy Spirit power. Let the oil of gladness rest upon me. I receive, today, Your divine enablement to fulfill the mission You have for my life. Give me the strength and might to overcome the enemy, to exercise Your authority in every situation, to see Your Kingdom come and Your will be done today. Overflow my life with Your fresh anointing Spirit. Empower me today to do your will.

## Luke 4:18

*The Spirit of the Lord is upon Me, because He has anointed Me To preach the gospel to the poor; He has sent Me to heal the brokenhearted, To proclaim liberty to the captives And recovery of sight to the blind, To set at liberty those who are oppressed.*

## Acts 1:8

*But you shall receive power when the Holy Spirit has come upon you; and you shall be witnesses to Me in Jerusalem, and in all Judea and Samaria, and to the end of the earth.*

## Acts 6:3

*Therefore, brethren, seek out from among you seven men of good reputation, full of the Holy Spirit and wisdom, whom we may appoint over this business;*

## Acts 9:17

*And Ananias went his way and entered the house; and laying his hands on him he said, "Brother Saul, the Lord Jesus, who appeared to you on the road as you came, has sent me that you may receive your sight and be filled with the Holy Spirit."*

## Acts 10:38

*How God anointed Jesus of Nazareth with the Holy Spirit and with power, who went about doing good and healing all who were oppressed by the devil, for God was with Him.*

## Zechariah 4:1-6

*Now the angel who talked with me came back and wakened me, as a man who is wakened out of his sleep. And he said to me, "What do you see?" So I said, "I am looking, and there is a lampstand of solid gold with a bowl on top of it, and on the stand seven lamps with seven pipes to the seven lamps. Two olive trees are by it, one at the right of the bowl and the other at its left." So I answered and spoke to the angel who talked with me, saying, "What are these, my lord?" Then the angel who talked with me answered and said to me, "Do you not know what these are?" And I said, "No, my lord." So he answered and said to me: "This is the word of the Lord to Zerubbabel: 'Not by might nor by power, but by My Spirit,' says the Lord of hosts.*

## *Isaiah 61:1-4*

*The Spirit of the Lord God is upon Me, Because the Lord has anointed Me To preach good tidings to the poor; He has sent Me to heal the brokenhearted, To proclaim liberty to the captives, And the opening of the prison to those who are bound; To proclaim the acceptable year of the Lord, And the day of vengeance of our God; To comfort all who mourn, To console those who mourn in Zion, To give them beauty for ashes, The oil of joy for mourning, The garment of praise for the spirit of heaviness; That they may be called trees of righteousness, The planting of the Lord, that He may be glorified." And they shall rebuild the old ruins, They shall raise up the former desolations, And they shall repair the ruined cities, The desolations of many generations.*

## *I Samuel 10:1*

*Then Samuel took a flask of oil and poured it on his head, and kissed him and said: "Is it not because the Lord has anointed you commander over His inheritance?*

## I Samuel 16:1

*Now the Lord said to Samuel, "How long will you mourn for Saul, seeing I have rejected him from reigning over Israel? Fill your horn with oil, and go; I am sending you to Jesse the Bethlehemite. For I have provided Myself a king among his sons."*

## Psalm 16:11

*You will show me the path of life; In Your presence is fullness of joy; At Your right hand are pleasures forevermore.*

## Psalm 45:7

*You love righteousness and hate wickedness; Therefore God, Your God, has anointed You With the oil of gladness more than Your companions.*

## Psalm 51:1

*Have mercy upon me, O God, According to Your lovingkindness; According to the multitude of Your tender mercies, Blot out my transgressions.*

## *Psalm 20:6*

*Now I know that the Lord saves His anointed; He will answer him from His holy heaven with the saving strength of His right hand.*

## *Psalm 28:8*

*The Lord is their strength, And He is the saving refuge of His anointed.*

## *Hebrews 1:9*

*You have loved righteousness and hated lawlessness; Therefore God, Your God, has anointed You With the oil of gladness more than Your companions."*

## *Exodus 33:14-16*

*And He said, "My Presence will go with you, and I will give you rest." Then he said to Him, "If Your Presence does not go with us, do not bring us up from here. For how then will it be known that Your people and I have found grace in Your sight, except You go with us? So we shall be separate, Your people and I, from all the people who are upon the face of the earth."*

## I John 2:20

*But you have an anointing from the Holy One, and you know all things... But the anointing which you have received from Him abides in you, and you do not need that anyone teach you; but as the same anointing teaches you concerning all things, and is true, and is not a lie, and just as it has taught you, you will abide in Him.*